Original title:
The Underwater Light

Copyright © 2025 Creative Arts Management OÜ
All rights reserved.

Author: Sebastian Whitmore
ISBN HARDBACK: 978-1-80587-333-4
ISBN PAPERBACK: 978-1-80587-803-2

## Secrets of the Abyssal Glow

A fish in a top hat, oh what a sight,
Waltzing with jellyfish, floating in plight.
They giggle and glimmer, in seaweed they twirl,
Making a splash in this watery whirl.

A clam plays the trumpet, what a strange band,
While octopi juggle with shells in their hand.
The sea cucumbers dance, not caring for rules,
While turtles take selfies, those quirky old fools.

## Beneath the Shimmering Surface

Anemones blush, oh so very shy,
As seahorses whisper and giggle nearby.
A parade of the oddballs, all here for the fun,
Trading their stories, their laughter's begun.

The crabs in their jackets, all spruced up with pride,
Offer a dance floor, where all fish can slide.
With bubbles as disco balls, making it glowy,
They party all night, just a bit too rowdy!

## Echoes of Radiance in Blue Depths

A dolphin with shades, oh so cool by the reef,
Says, "Life's a splash party, beyond any belief!"
With groupers as bodyguards, they guard the fun,
While octopus breakdance, oh, they're number one!

They chuckle and snicker as the stingrays glide,
Belly laughs echo through the currents they ride.
With rays of bright humor, they illuminate waves,
In the land of the giggles, where everyone raves.

## Flickers of Hope in Ocean Shadows

A starfish in slippers hops 'round on the floor,
Kicking up seaweed while shouting, "More, more!"
The clownfish are chuckling in stripes of bright hue,
Painting the ocean with laughter anew.

Each bubble that rises is a giggle released,
From creatures who know how to party at least.
With laughter and bubbles, they dance through the night,
In this world of wonders, where the funny takes flight.

**Glows from the Forgotten Trenches**

In darkened nooks, the critters jig,
With disco moves, they dance and wig.
A fish in shades of neon pink,
Sips seaweed smoothies, takes a wink.

Tickled by the bubbles' cheer,
The octopus spins, oh what a seer!
A clam is flipping pancakes wide,
With shrimp as chefs, they take great pride.

A crab with shades strolls with flair,
While jellyfish float without a care.
In trenches deep, the party's bright,
Where every glow brings pure delight.

So if you find, in ocean's sway,
A raving school of fish at play,
Dive right in, join the parade,
In the deep sea's fun, don't be afraid!

## Fathoms of Flickering Hope

They say the depths hold secrets dear,
But here, creatures laugh and cheer.
A starfish juggling shells with grace,
While turtles crack jokes, keeping pace.

A barnacle band strikes up the tune,
Playing sonatas beneath the moon.
With tuneful bubbles as their guide,
They'll tickle your fins; come enjoy the ride!

The squids throw ink like confetti bright,
A spectacle seen in the dark of night.
Clownfish chuckle as they pirouette,
These underwater pals are quite a pet!

So paddle down to the coral's dome,
Join the laughter, it feels like home.
In depths where joy is fully scoped,
You'll find the glow of flickering hope.

## The Sea's Hidden Fireflies

In the kelp forest, a glow is found,
With flitting lights that whirl around.
Tiny critters buzzing with glee,
Like underwater fireflies, wild and free.

A grouper grins with a wink, oh dear,
Chasing glowsticks through the gear.
While sea sponges tumble like silly fools,
Learning how to groove with the schools.

A lanternfish plays hide and seek,
With calamari, who squeak and peek.
All while a dolphin organizes a race,
Flipping and splashing with joyous grace.

So gather 'round the dazzling crew,
With friends like these, there's much to do.
In the sea where laughter shines wide,
The hidden fireflies will be your guide.

## **Twilight in the Tidal Kin**

As twilight dips in ocean's sway,
Crabs wear hats and boogie all day.
A sea cucumber sports a bow tie,
While fish don dresses, oh my my!

The tide pools echo with joyous shouts,
Starry night bringing laughter bouts.
A whale pulls pranks with a splashy twist,
While eels wiggle in a funky mist.

The barnacles gossip in the dark,
As pulsing lights ignite a spark.
The creatures spin, twirl, and glide,
In tidal kin, let joy abide.

So wade right in, don't miss the fun,
With every joke, a laugh is spun.
In twilight's glow with friends galore,
You'll never long for the sandy shore!

## **Dances of Bioluminescent Dreams**

In the depths where fish wear glow,
They jig and sway, putting on a show.
With fins that flash like disco balls,
Even crustaceans join the calls.

Jellyfish twirl in a jelly waltz,
A slippery dance, full of faults.
Shrimp do the cha-cha, bouncing proud,
Bubbles pop, and they laugh out loud.

Octopuses spin with eight-legged flair,
In this aquatic club, they've no care.
Seaweed sways to their jigging beat,
A party where all creatures meet.

As the night rolls on, squids draw near,
With color shows that draw a cheer.
In this splashy, glowing, fishy scene,
The underwater dance floor reigns supreme!

## Echoes of the Ocean's Heart

Beneath the waves, the chuckles rise,
As fish trade jokes in bright disguise.
Anemones giggle, clinging tight,
At something strange that swims in sight.

A dolphin tells a cracking pun,
While turtles munch on algae fun.
Starfish snicker, waving their arms,
While crabs share secrets and silly charms.

Whales hum tunes with wobbly notes,
As their playful echoes gently float.
With bubbles bursting, laughter spreads,
Making merry in their watery beds.

As the tide rolls in, the sea donkeys bray,
"Who needs land when we can play?"
These echoes from the ocean's core,
Are hilarity, forevermore!

**Celestial Beacons Beneath the Waves**

Little critters shine like stars,
Carried on currents, no need for cars.
Tiny lanterns in a sea parade,
Swaying with joy, never afraid.

Crabs in tuxedos strut with pride,
While oysters giggle and try to hide.
A sea cucumber wobbles with flair,
In this glow, nobody has a care.

Flashing light as a beacon calls,
Even anglerfish have giggling brawls.
Attracting pals with a wink and a flick,
They throw a party, with bubbles, they kick!

With each glimmer, the sea bursts bright,
A cosmic scene, pure delight.
In this flickering glow, best friends unite,
Making waves of laughter into the night!

## Glistening Whispers of the Abyss

In the depths where shadows play,
Whispers dance and sway away.
A fish with disco dreams and schemes,
Glows bright as if to join our themes.

Tangled kelp echoes laughter's sound,
As bubbles giggle, surfacing round.
With whispers soft as ocean's breath,
Humor floats in the watery depth.

A hefty whale quips and grins wide,
Dropping beats from the vast tide.
Clownfish chuckle with bright-painted cheeks,
In this realm where joy quietly speaks.

When darkness falls and all seems lost,
The glowing secrets come at a cost.
For laughter rings through every wave,
In glistening whispers, we all behave!

## Ephemeral Glows in Dark Edges

In depths where fish wear suits of glee,
A jellyfish does a jig for me.
With tentacles like party streamers,
It twirls and swirls—what a thinker!

Bubble-blowers of the briny sea,
Pufferfish puffed up, quite the spree.
They share their secrets in a sigh,
As seaweed giggles, drifting by.

A clam claps once, a clam claps twice,
Telling tales of terrible spice.
Once pranked a shark with a fake pearl,
Now laughs abound in this aquatic swirl.

Shrimp tap dance on the ocean bed,
As sea cucumbers shake their head.
A starfish shimmies in bright confetti,
All while an octopus wears a beanie.

## **Winking Souls of the Ocean Floor**

The sea floor comes alive at night,
With creatures winking, what a sight!
A crab in glasses, reading the sea,
Tells jokes that tickle, just for me.

Angelfish gossip, fluttering fins,
While seahorses twirl and spin.
A shark plays tag, a game of gig,
That leaves little minnows feeling big.

Anemones sway in bright ballet,
With tiny shrimp that jump and play.
They laugh and tease in a splashy sport,
While bubbles rise like the best consort.

Octopuses juggle pearls with flair,
Each drop a chuckle, a watery dare.
In this grand show beneath the waves,
We dance with delight as the ocean raves.

## **Surfaces of a Glimmering Dreamscape**

The waves are giggling, tickled and bright,
Where sunlight splashes in pure delight.
A clownfish honks, in pastel hues,
Wearing mismatched, silly shoes.

Glimmers and glances, a playful tease,
As sea turtles glide with the greatest of ease.
They flip and flop, with goofy grins,
In the splashy party the ocean spins.

Starry-eyed squids paint the black,
Drawing mustaches on every back.
With bursts of color—a curious sight,
They giggle and dance in the shimmering light.

A dolphin pops up to share a rhyme,
With a joke that could make seaweed climb.
In this realm of radiant cheer,
Every splash echoes—a laugh loud and clear.

## Where Shadows Dance with Light

In shadows where the seaweed grows,
Sea otters wrap in kelp like bows.
Happily tickling one another,
Rolling and laughing all in cover.

Crabs open up an evening show,
With jokes that make the barnacles glow.
They shuffle and giggle, quite absurd,
As mussels applaud without a word.

A fish with a top hat states its claim,
To lead an underwater game.
As others join in with a splashy cheer,
They whirl around with no sign of fear.

Bubbles burst and laughter spread,
In this dark place where joy is bred.
From depths unknown to the ocean's crest,
Every creature knows how to jest.

## Rippled Radiance in Submarine Vistas

In the depths where fish like disco balls,
They shimmy and shake, ignoring the calls.
A crab with a hat struts by with delight,
While octopuses twirl in the glow of the night.

Bubbles pop like party favors galore,
As seaweed sways, eager for more.
A goldfish with shades, looking quite cool,
Sipped sea foam smoothies, 'cause that's how they rule.

**Ethereal Twinkles in the Coral Garden**

In a coral jungle, where colors clash bright,
A starfish is juggling with all of its might.
Clownfish are laughing, they're masters of jokes,
While a dolphin nearby just can't stand the pokes.

Anemones wave, like they're on a parade,
While seahorses dance in a fine masquerade.
A snail in a shell sings off-key with a grin,
Fish all around say, 'Let the fun begin!'

## When Darkness Dances with Light

In the gloom where shadows form curious shapes,
A squid tells tall tales, while the turtle escapes.
A lanternfish winks, like it knows all the cues,
While eels in their costumes put on quite the blues.

A searchlight shines down, oh what a grand sight!
As shrimp hold a contest for who's most contrite.
Cuttlefish giggle, blending in with the show,
They paint the dark world, putting on quite a glow.

## Shimmering Hues Beneath Tall Waves

In shimmering waters where silly things dwell,
A whale sings a tune with a loud, funny yell.
Dancing in bubbles, a flounder does twirl,
While a parrotfish paints its deck with a whirl.

A pufferfish puffed up, looks ready to burst,
Claims it's a balloon, and it's feeling dispersed.
With a wink and a giggle, it floats on its way,
Saying, 'Catch me if you can, it's a fishy ballet!'

### **Distant Gleams in the Marine Veil**

Bubbles rise with a giggle,
Fish in tuxedos start to wiggle.
A crab confuses his left for right,
Dancing along in the shimmering light.

Octopus wearing a party hat,
Spinning around like a playful cat.
Jellyfish glow, they float and sway,
Join the throng for a silly ballet.

**Riddles of the Deep's Light.**

A turtle thinks he's a wise old sage,
Reading seaweed like it's a page.
Pufferfish chuckle, with cheeks all puffed,
While shrimp try to get their dance moves snuffed.

Clams hold meetings, all in a shell,
Trading secrets, oh, what tales they tell!
Anemones giggle, tangled in threads,
While starfish compare their luminous spreads.

## Dancing in Aquatic Glimmer

A seal with shades, he strikes a pose,
Balancing pearls on his toes.
Dolphins leap, they twirl and spin,
Synchronized swimming with a cheeky grin.

Seahorses strut in a conga line,
Wiggling their tails — isn't it fine?
Frogs in the sea trying to croak,
What a laugh when they play a joke!

## Luminescent Whispers Beneath the Waves

Starry wonders from the ocean's bed,
Whispers of laughter where fish tread.
Crabs sing loudly in a squeaky tone,
While oysters gossip in a sparkling zone.

Anglerfish flaunt their glowing bait,
Fishing for puns — isn't that great?
With every flash, a giggle is spun,
In this watery world, there's always fun!

## **Luminous Tales of the Deep Blue**

Down in the briny, fish wear shades,
While jellyfish dance in glittering parades.
A clam plays the drums, a shrimp sings a tune,
As sea cucumbers groove by the light of the moon.

Octopuses juggle their eight floppy arms,
Impressing the dolphins with their silly charms.
Clownfish chuckle, oh what a sight,
Trying to tango in the shimmer so bright.

The seahorses twirl in the bubble-wrap breeze,
Each tickle and splash can bring forth a sneeze.
With laughter as bubbles, they rise to the top,
And the giggling waves seem to never quite stop.

So come take a peek at this whimsical show,
Where the deep sea jesters put on quite a glow.
In this cavern of whimsy, the joy's never brief,
Just keep your fins ready for a ticklish reef!

## **Whispers from the Ocean's Prism**

Bubbles are giggling, the octopuses jest,
While starfish play cards, they're always the best.
A walrus with glasses plays chess with a crab,
And sea turtles wink from their smart little lab.

In coral like candy, the clownfish convene,
Telling tall tales about seas that they've seen.
Anemones chuckle as they sway to the beat,
Tickling a grouper that can't find his seat.

A shrimp with a bow tie, so dapper and spry,
Challenges seagulls to a dance in the sky.
The waves arch and bubble, their laughter in tow,
Shooting stars from the ocean do a dive in the flow.

And down in the depths where the laughter is grand,
They serve jellybean cocktails from the softest of sand.
So trust in the whispers that echo and gleam,
For the ocean's a stage and it's funnier than it seems!

## Twilight hues beneath the tides

In twilight's embrace, a fish band arrives,
With fins as their instruments, they harmonize.
A catfish conductor waves his long wiggly tail,
While crabs do the cha-cha and never go pale.

Anemones blush in the soft, glowing haze,
As flounders play tag in a merry malaise.
The sea snail's a poet, reciting his verse,
While the friendly old tuna just rolls with a curse.

Dolphins dive high, then come crashing back down,
Where seaweed gets tangled and starts to frown.
"Why are we here?" asks a wise little guppy,
As they all splash about finding things oh-so-happy.

So listen close, friend, to their giggly delight,
For the sea holds a party from dawn until night.
In hues of soft twilight, they carelessly glide,
Dancing in rhythm, let laughter be your guide!

## Reflections of Celestial Beams

A starfish who dreams of being a star,
Wishes on bubbles that float from afar.
"Turn me to stardust," he giggles with glee,
As he bounces around, all jolly and free.

A cheeky fish checks his scales in the sea,
Wondering if he's more shimmery than me.
He poses for selfies with rocks as his crew,
While krill all applaud with "Bravo! Well, woo!"

The moon's got a wink for the tides on their way,
Painting silver-lined waves that frolic and sway.
With each splash and twirl, they throw sparkles around,
As the seabed hears laughter, a jubilant sound.

So don't be too serious when diving in deep,
The night's filled with magic, in dreams we can leap.
With reflections of joy and some giggles galore,
The world underwater is never a bore!

## Ghostly Flickers of the Sea

In the depths where fish sing tunes,
There are sparkles that play with the moons.
A jellyfish floats, doing a jig,
While a clam plays piano, oh so big!

An octopus tells jokes, it's true,
With eight arms waving just for you.
The seaweed giggles, sways to the beat,
As crabs in tuxedos tap their feet!

A treasure chest seemed so shy,
Until a starfish made it fly.
They twirled and swirled, a dance so merry,
With sea cucumbers joining, looking very!

So join this party, don't be late,
Where bubbles are laughter, oh what a fate!
Under the waves, the fun won't cease,
In this ghostly flicker, find pure peace!

## Hidden Brilliance in Coral Caverns

Below the waves where secrets stay,
Coral reefs have games to play.
With fish in tuxedos and bright bow ties,
They host a soirée that never dies!

Anemones flirt like winks of light,
While a seahorse says, 'Aren't I a sight?'
The pufferfish pops, a balloon gone wrong,
Yet the parrotfish sings the jolliest song!

Crabs look on, with claws raised high,
Judging dances as the currents sigh.
A clam plays charades with the hermit crab crew,
Their shenanigans spark laughter anew!

Deep in the caverns, it's a riot unseen,
With bioluminescence painted so keen.
Join in the fun, let your cares drift away,
In hidden brilliance, brighten your day!

## **A Dance with Mermaid's Glow**

Mermaids twirl in a seaweed swirl,
With shells and pearls, they give a twirl.
Their giggles echo, enchanting and bright,
As fish dance along, a humorous sight!

A dolphin joins, doing flips and spins,
Saying, 'Who knew sea life could have wins?'
They cartwheel through bubbles, laughter huge,
While sea snails sing, it's quite the deluge!

In shimmering waters, they share their tales,
With starfish wranglers, who ride tiny whales.
A crab comically acts like a boss,
As everyone giggles, no one feels loss.

So swim with glee in this watery show,
With every wink from the mermaids' glow.
You'll find the fun beneath the waves,
In a dance so bright, your heart it saves!

## Echoing Color in Marine Silence

In the quiet depths, colors collide,
A rainbow fish parade, much to your pride.
They honk like a horn, oh what a sound,
As bubbles pop, laughter resounds!

A turtle drifts with a giggly grin,
Playing hide and seek with an octopus twin.
They slip and slide on a sea sponge floor,
While the clownfish roll, needing no encore!

Waterfalls echo with bright chirps all around,
As creatures take selfies, laughter unbound.
In this silent world where colors scheme,
They paint a picture, a joyful dream!

So dive into this fun, don't be shy,
Where marine silence is a gleeful sigh.
Each echoing color, a story untold,
In this watery world, find joy manifold!

## **Visionary Depths of Submerged Luminescence**

In the ocean's grand ballet, fish wear suits so bright,
Jellybeans float by, glowing with delight.
Octopus in top hats, dancing with a flair,
"Who's the best-dressed cephalopod?" they declare.

Seahorses in visors wave from their coral chair,
Sipping on seaweed smoothies, without a care.
The snails are in a contest, slow and steady wins,
While clams start a rumor, who wears the best fins?

Nautilus has a twinkle, shows off with a spin,
"Check out my new shell!" he calls, full of grin.
The sea floor's a runway, shells and scales so bright,
Every creature dressing up for the dazzling night!

Bubble parties erupt, filled with giggles and glee,
Whales make the best DJs, oh how they move free!
With every wave's rhythm, the laughter takes flight,
In this world of glow and humor, everything's light!

## The Glow of Forgotten Seas

Deep in the old trenches, the fish tell their tales,
Of pirates and treasures with shiny scales.
A crab with a monocle plays captain so proud,
While starfish direct traffic, waving arms loud.

Anemones dress up, all frills and no fuss,
"Do you think I look pretty?" they ask with a blush.
The eels share the gossip beneath swaying kelp,
"Did you hear about Paul, he's gone and found help!"

Ghostly ships whisper secrets; the seahorse takes notes,
While dolphins flip out in their luminous coats.
An old clam sings blues in a style so rare,
Every note is a chuckle that floats through the air.

As sea cucumbers shuffle through algae and grime,
The laughter grows louder, it's party old-time!
Every dive brings more joy, they dance and they jest,
In the glow of forgotten seas, they're truly the best!

## **Glimpses of Light Among Coral Shadows**

In coral reefs, secrets hide in bright cheeky tubes,
Clownfish play pranks, inviting the moods.
A grouper tells jokes while polishing his scales,
"Why don't fish play cards? They're afraid of the gales!"

Turtles with shades cruise the aquatic scene,
"Look at those bright fish, are they also on screen?"
Tangs spin in circles, leave swirls in their wake,
While feather-dusters sway, saying, "For goodness' sake!"

A hidden crab whispers, "I've got quite a hunch,
There's a party tonight. Hey, wanna join for lunch?"
With flashes of color, they join in the spree,
Where laughter bubbles up in a wild jubilee.

Encounters with giggles and jubilant glee,
Each flicker of light is a reason to be.
Among coral shadows, the fun never sets,
In this underwater kingdom, no one has regrets!

## Luring Light Beneath Ocean Waves

Beneath the cool waves, a glow starts to tease,
Fish gather in circles, easy as you please.
A lanternfish giggles, "I shine like a star!"
While krill have a dance-off, not caring by far.

The glow-worms are shining, with bling on their tails,
"Who wore it better? The puffer or snails?"
A shrimp stacks up pearls, "Look at my own bling!
They say less is more, but I'm doing my thing!"

Electric rays swim, light up the whole show,
"Join us for some frolic!" they beckon below.
While snug in their homes, the shy octopi peek,
Wondering if tonight's the night they will speak!

In this underwater cabaret, all's full of cheer,
Where laughter is woven, and fun is sincere.
Among bubbles and sparkles, they sway and they play,
Luring each other beneath the bright waves' ballet!

## Murmurs of the Glimmering Deep

Bubbles dance and fish all sway,
As seaweed sings a little play.
Crabs do the cha-cha with such flair,
While jellybeans float without a care.

Octopus juggles some shiny shells,
Pufferfish giggle and tell their tales.
Turtle wears shades like a rockstar king,
As sea stars laugh, they do their thing.

The clownfish jokes, oh what a sight,
Tickling sea cucumbers with delight.
A conch shell whispers secrets so grand,
While laughing eels join in the band.

Waves come crashing, a bubbly show,
Underwater joy, a vibrant glow.
All the sea critters dance in delight,
In this happy world, everything's bright.

## Enchantment in the Watery Veil

Mermaids giggle with watery grace,
While turtles race in a gentle chase.
Anemones tickle, oh what a prank,
In produce aisle colors of green and plank.

Angelfish strut with their finest dress,
Adding some shimmer, they make quite a mess.
A dolphin flips, creating a splash,
While sea horses dangle, oh what a clash!

The sea's a party, it's never dull,
With krill and shrimp and a bright orange skull.
Every creature, from big to small,
Is bursting with laughter; it's a ball!

At twilight's call, the bubbles rise,
A confetti of sparkles under the skies.
Finny fun in this magical place,
Where joy and laughter never leave a trace.

## **Deep-Sea Stars and Their Stories**

Starfish tell tales of undersea fright,
Of rogue waves and kraken fights at night.
Clownfish chuckle at tales a bit tall,
Dressed like jesters, they rule the hall.

Whales hum songs that shake the ground,
While glowing plankton twirl all around.
An old boot becomes a treasure chest,
In this watery world full of jest.

Sea urchins poke with a curious flair,
While lobsters tap dance, they're quite rare.
Coral enthrones the gossiping friends,
With laughter and fun that never ends.

So gather the crew for some salty cheer,
Dive deep in the joy and let out a cheer.
In the depths of the sea, let's spin and swirl,
For smiling and giggles make the ocean twirl.

## Radiant Horizons Beneath the Surface

In shimmering depths, the antics unfold,
With goldfish gossip in bubbles of gold.
The hermit crabs strut with homes on their backs,
While clams snap jokes in their cozy stacks.

Locusts leap, but where do they go?
In the fished-out waters, there's a show!
A fish in a tux, oh what a sight,
Waltzing through coral, oh what delight!

The sea anemone tickles and spins,
While barnacles chuckle, oh what grins.
Seahorses wag their tails with flair,
While dancing past kelp, so light as air.

So raise up a fin to this silly scene,
Where laughter and bubbles make all routines.
Beneath hues of aqua, endless and bright,
We swim in giggles and joy, pure delight.

**Radiant Secrets from the Abyss**

In the depths where fish do dance,
With glowing smiles, they prance.
A jellyfish in a wig so bright,
Swings around in sheer delight.

An octopus wears a silly hat,
Teasing crabs that look like that!
The treasure chest sings a tune,
While a sea turtle dances to the moon.

Sardines form a sparkling band,
Playing tunes on barnacle land.
A clam tried to join the scene,
But its shell was far too green!

So here beneath the waves we see,
A party full of glee and spree.
With creatures bright and colors bold,
Underwater wonders to behold!

## Undersea Citadels of Glimmering Light

In castles made of coral seams,
Fish throw parties, bursting beams.
With disco balls of bubbles near,
They shimmy, shudder, spread good cheer.

A crab serves snacks on silver platters,
While fishy gossip, oh how it scatters!
A glowing prince with fins so rare,
Tells jokes that leave you gasping air.

A sea cucumber does a twirl,
While dolphins spin and leap and whirl.
Each wave a tune that flows with fun,
Undersea parties never shun!

So raise a shell to ocean's flair,
Where laughter echoes everywhere.
With lights that twinkle like the stars,
In the deep—no need for cars!

## **Shining Through Aquatic Murk**

Beneath the waves where shadows play,
A clownfish seeks to find its way.
With glowing friends, it starts to shine,
A disco ball? Oh, never mine!

Anglerfish holds a dinner show,
Inviting all, and off they go!
Each fin a sparkle, every scale,
A party where no one can fail.

The seaweed grooves like it's alive,
As giggles spark and dolphins dive.
A conch-shell singer belts a tune,
Filling hearts with underwater swoon!

Together they frolic, splash, and play,
Bright bulbs turning night into day.
In murky depths, the fun won't cease,
Where joy and laughter swim with ease!

## Threads of Light in the Mesopelagic

In layers deep, where dark things dart,
The fish are bold and play their part.
With lanterns strapped upon each head,
They light the way as jokes are spread.

A shimmering squid makes silly faces,
While absurd sea spiders claim their spaces.
Each glow a laugh, each flicker a jest,
These silly critters are the best!

A blubberfish bursts out in song,
Its bubbles rise, a merry throng.
The angler calls for one more dance,
As creatures turn and twirl in trance.

So dance beneath the waves so bright,
Where every smile brings pure delight.
In depths so dark, we find our cheer,
With glowing friends and tunes we hear!

## Elysian Gloam Beneath Waves

In the deep, fish wear hats,
Sipping bubbles, great chats!
Octopus juggles his lunch,
Makes everyone laugh, what a punch!

Coral reefs dance in tunes,
Tickling sea urchins with marooned spoons.
Starfish play cards with no hands,
Betting on shells from distant sands!

Jellyfish glide in fuzzy socks,
They're the kings of fun, no locks!
Anemones throw a confetti blast,
As crabs breakdance, they've got some sass!

Undersea disco, they jump and twirl,
Pufferfish jesters, in a free-for-all swirl.
The ocean's a party, come take a dive,
In this realm of laughter, we're all alive!

## Songs of the Light-Gorged Depths

Bubble-blowers, singing glee,
Turtles doing the conga, oh wee!
Clownfish cracking jokes on a reef,
Laughter bounces, beyond belief!

Seahorses gallop, quite absurd,
Shaking it off, a dance unheard.
They twirl and spin with such delight,
As seaweed wiggles, a playful sight!

Whales conduct an underwater band,
With sea cucumber shakers, quite grand!
They play the tunes of the deep blue,
Making waves, oh what a view!

Starry skies look down and grin,
As fish wear wigs and spin for a win.
Ocean's laughter, a bubbling song,
In this watery world, you can't go wrong!

## Glimmering Veils of the Sea

There's a dance-off with sea slugs,
In glittery veils, they pull sweet hugs.
A seal keeps time, clapping his fins,
As the seaweed sways, laughter begins!

Clams are a bit shy, but they clap,
While fish wear their best, taking a nap.
Urchins are bouncing, what a sight,
Under the shimmery waves, pure delight!

A grouper struts in flashy shoes,
While jellybeans cheer with silly views.
The water sparkles like a dream,
Where silliness reigns, and giggles gleam!

With barnacles joining in the fun,
Sardines spin as they run!
Veils of laughter, floating all day,
In the glimmering sea, we laugh away!

## Lost Light in the Depths

Where dim fish get lost in thought,
And sea cucumbers joke, feeling caught.
Eels tell tales of long-lost socks,
While sponge bob-comics fill the docks!

Anemones grumble, 'Where's the glow?'
As turtles giggle, 'Just go with the flow!'
Crustaceans joke about evening snacks,
With pinchy claws and colorful packs!

Bubbles burst with ticklish squeals,
While mackerels brush up on their reels.
Frolicking fishes, such a sight,
In the depths where there's lost light!

Squid unveil their comedy, a show,
As they squirt ink for an extra glow.
Underneath the waves, lollybobs play,
In the depths of laughter, we all sway!

## Fantasies Wrapped in Radiance

In depths where bubbles giggle and play,
Bright creatures dance in a curious ballet,
An octopus shows off its vibrant new dress,
While jellyfish laugh in a glowing excess.

A turtle sings songs of his ancient fame,
While starfish compete to join in the game,
With a flick of a fin, they twirl and they spin,
In a world where the silly takes root from within.

Sea cucumbers ponder their squishy old fate,
While fish share gossip about their last date,
The coral reefs chuckle, a riot of hues,
Creating a symphony, bursting with blues.

A seahorse twirls on a bubble-shaped swing,
As clams make sounds like they're starting to sing,
In this underwater realm, what a delight,
Where laughter abounds in the shimmering night.

## Tales of the Deep's Hidden Glow

In twilight waters where the silliness thrives,
Fish tell tall tales of their dazzling dives,
The anglerfish grins with a whimsical tease,
While manta rays glide with elegant ease.

Crabs in tuxedos are ready to dance,
As seaweed sways in a mischievous trance,
Anemones giggle, swishing about,
In this realm where chuckles root out any doubt.

Dolphins leap high, bringing joy to the dark,
As narwhals play chess with a deep-sea shark,
The treasure chests hide their sparkly gems,
While funny fish wink from their coral stems.

A pufferfish tries on a comical hat,
With a flamboyant flair, oh, imagine that!
Bubbles of laughter rise up to the top,
In these stories of whimsy, they never will stop.

## **Reflections of Marine Luminosity**

Beneath the waves, where the colors ignite,
A school of fish beams in radiant flight,
With neon fins, they spin and they whirl,
Creating a show that makes laughter unfurl.

A walrus jokes about its mustache so grand,
While seals stack up, forming a funny band,
The roofs of the ocean shine bright in the gloom,
As giggles and chuckles boom through the room.

In clamshell theaters, the acts never cease,
With bubble-blowing whales that bring laughter and peace,
The seascape is filled with joy and delight,
In their glowing embrace, all worries take flight.

As mermaids host parties, oh what a sight,
With sea turtles serving up snacks for the night,
In this whimsical world where the silly takes sway,
They dance with abandon, come join in the play!

## Glistening Heartbeats of the Deep

In a sea where fish wear shades,
A jellyfish dance with prancy parades.
Octopuses giggle at silly plays,
While crabs do the cha-cha in sandy bays.

A starfish winks, oh what a sight!
As bubbles giggle in sheer delight.
Seahorses twirl in a wobbly race,
Just don't ask them to keep up pace.

Clownfish juggle with seaweed rings,
Playing catch with all of their flings.
They form a band, it's quite a show,
With corals clapping, "Let's go, let's go!"

Anemones sway, soft rockstars they are,
While turtles munch popcorn, oh how bizarre!
In depths of the sea, heartbeats do gleam,
A comical dream in a jelly-filled stream.

## The Whisper of Glow Beneath

Down below where shadows play,
Bubbles chuckle in a giddy ballet.
Starry squids tell tales of old,
With glow-in-the-dark smiles, bright and bold.

Shrimp in tuxedos, dancing parade,
In their frosty ocean masquerade.
A dolphin dons a sunny hat,
Chasing fish, "Just look at that!"

Turtles with ties that float and sway,
Join in the laughter, "What a day!"
Coral reefs echo a whimsical tune,
While sea cucumbers croon under the moon.

Even a clam gets a joke or two,
"Oysters, you won't believe who flew!"
In this fun abyss, where glee knows no end,
The whispers of glow are the sea's best friend.

## Echoes of Light in Coral Kingdoms

In kingdoms where corals blush and beam,
Fish wear sun hats and lollygaggle like a dream.
Clownfish are jesters with their funny quips,
While parrotfish giggle, rolling on their lips.

A crab in a car has taken a ride,
He honks at the clowns that dance by the tide.
Tropical frogs croon their favorite song,
Making sure the conchs hum along all day long.

Angelfish share glittery gossip with glee,
While glittery dazies swim around carefree.
Dolphins make waves that sparkle and twirl,
As hilarity spreads through this aquatic swirl.

Jellyfish play peek-a-boo, oh what a scene,
With giggles and wiggles, they twirl and careen.
In this sea of echoes, laughter takes flight,
A wacky wonderland, oh, what a sight!

## **Drenched in Aquatic Brilliance**

In waters swirling with shimmering cheer,
Goldfish tell tales that tickle the ear.
A narwhal spins like a disco ball,
Bringing laughter to every sea hull and hall.

Tangs wear tuxes, ready to prance,
While seaweed does the sway and dance.
"Do the fish flip!" the clam snickers loud,
As an octopus nods, feeling quite proud.

Each ray beams joy with a funky twist,
While squids paint the walls, you get the gist.
Mollusks make jokes about fishy affairs,
While everyone laughs with salty flares.

In glossy depths, where smiles ignite,
Creatures unite in blissful delight.
Drenched in a glow so sparkling bright,
The ocean's a stages where humor takes flight.

## What Lies Beneath the Luminous Surface

In a world where fish wear shorts,
Bubbles dance like playful cohorts.
Crabs play cards with a wink and grin,
While squids juggle pearls with a spin.

Starfish gossip about the sun,
"We're the best, oh, this is fun!"
A turtle on a surfboard rides,
Waving to folks in ocean tides.

## **Lighthouses of the Deep Blue**

A jellyfish runs a light café,
Coffee served in a seaweed tray.
A shark in shades, he sips his brew,
While dolphins laugh and dance in queue.

Crabs bake cookies in fiery spots,
But they avoid those tricky knots.
Octopus chefs cook with a flair,
Whipping up dishes beyond compare.

## Secrets of the Glimmering Deep

Mermaids sport stylish evening gowns,
Lobsters tipping their lavender crowns.
Seahorses waltz on the ocean floor,
Telling tales of fishy folklore.

Anemones host the cutest show,
With clams as stars, they steal the glow.
A whale hums tunes that tickle the soul,
While fishy friends perform rock 'n roll.

**Navigating Through Radiant Waterways**

A crew of turtles play hide and seek,
Each shell is a secret, bright and unique.
Seashells crack jokes that echo for miles,
While squids engage in silly trials.

Pufferfish strut with their spiky might,
Waving hello, they're quite the sight.
As starfish twirl in a silly trance,
Everything sways to an underwater dance.

## Reflections in the Midnight Tide

In the depths where the fish do wink,
Jellyfish dance and dolphins think.
With a flick of a tail, they shine so bright,
While seaweed giggles in the twilight.

Starfish juggling, oh what a sight!
Crabs in tuxedos, feeling just right.
A clam starts to sing a tuneful jig,
Even octopuses join in, big and sprig!

The lobster waves with a happy cheer,
While seahorses strut, oh so sincere.
In this underwater festive spree,
Who knew the ocean could hold a tea?

## Navigating through Aquatic Lanterns

Waves of laughter ripple and splash,
As fish make jokes and crabs do a dash.
Navigating with glee, what a delight,
Finding treasures that shimmer, so bright.

A pufferfish dons a ballooned crown,
Making silly faces, never a frown.
With octopus arms, he'll stand for a trick,
Tickling the mermaid, oh what a kick!

The sea cucumber plays hide and seek,
Hiding away, oh so very meek.
But with a tickle from a nearby shrimp,
They burst out laughing, swimming in the limpid blimp!

**Veils of Aquatic Radiance**

Corals whisper secrets, oh so bold,
In colors that shimmer, bright and gold.
The clownfish joke in their playful lair,
With fins that flutter like they just don't care.

Underneath the waves, anemones sway,
Waving at fish who dance and play.
Turtles twirl, escaping a chase,
All whilst donning a comical face!

The sunbeams paint a glimmering tune,
Fish croon along like they're meeting the moon.
With bubbles that giggle, oh what a thrill,
The ocean's a carnival, and time stands still!

## Illuminated Shadows of the Sea

Shadows jiggle in the soft, blue glow,
A friendly whale puts on quite a show.
Tickled by bubbles in the darkest brine,
Octopi giggle, 'How clever's this line!'

Fishes in tuxedos, fancy yet wild,
Joking about swimming like a child.
With a wink and a swish, they play tag at night,
In this ball of the sea, everything's light.

Underneath the waves, the laughter thrives,
Dancing with currents and making high dives.
Jellyfish float as they spin around,
In this watery world, joy knows no bound.

## **Beneath the Ripple's Glow**

Fish wear hats and dance around,
Clams tell jokes, oh what a sound!
Crabs do the cha-cha, an underwater spree,
While seaweed sways like a funky tree.

Jellyfish bounce with their see-through pride,
Squids juggle shells, a comical ride.
Octopus chefs whip up tasty bites,
In their bubbly kitchen, under shimmering lights.

Dolphins giggle, making splashes wide,
Echoing laughter in the ocean's tide.
A starfish spins tales of the great big sea,
As turtles join in, full of glee.

So come dive down where the fun won't stop,
Under the waves, it's a non-stop bop.
With silliness swirling like bubbles in air,
Join this party, if you dare!

**Secrets of the Deep Blue**

Waves peak like laughter, bubbling with cheer,
Secret tales whispered for those who come near.
Ladyfish flaunt their sparkly fins,
As clownfish joke about making sins.

In hidden nooks, the gobies can sing,
To a raucous tune, the eels start to swing.
With sea cucumbers cracking wise,
They roll with the punch, oh what a surprise!

The turtles hold court, cracking up foes,
While a pufferfish blows to make funny poses.
Shrimps clink glasses made out of shells,
Toast to the tales that the ocean swells.

The secret's out, and there's no going back,
The deep blue's laughter fills every crack.
Join in the fun, it's a splashy delight,
In the heart of the waves, everything's bright!

## Luminescence in the Abyss

In twilight depths, where the giggles thrive,
Glow-worms chuckle, keeping dreams alive.
Anglerfish flaunt their lights with a wink,
Casting giggles, letting the shadows rethink.

A goblin shark grins with a toothy smile,
Letting the sea critters giggle a while.
Crabs turn the tide with slapstick flair,
Dodging their foes without a single care.

A phantom reshapes the stories we know,
With beams of humor that steal the show.
As deep sea daisies do a little jig,
There's fun to be found, in every big gig!

So dive into darkness, where joy can reside,
In luminous waters, let laughter be the guide.
You'll find the abyss hides more than just fright,
It sparkles with silliness, day and night!

## **Shimmers of Forgotten Depths**

Forgotten treasures, in boxes of foam,
Dancing with joy as they dream of their home.
A sunken ship holds a party in style,
The barnacles join in, all wearing a smile.

Merfolk are laughing, weaving grand tales,
With waves as their stage, they'll never grow stale.
Barnacles chanting in a chorus so grand,
Singing of frolics in a whimsical band.

Blowfish burst with laughter, puffing with pride,
As anemones sway, they're never denied.
Each flicker and shimmer, a glimpse of delight,
In the depths of the ocean, everything's bright!

So come to this kingdom, let your heart soar!
Join in the laughter, there's always much more.
In forgotten depths where the fun's on display,
Dive into giggles and swim the day away!

## Shards of Light in Aquatic Realms

Bubbles giggle as they form,
Little fish dance and perform.
Jellyfish flashing like a clue,
What's that glow? Just me in a shoe!

Seahorses twirl, their tails a swirl,
They play tag while the seaweed twirls.
An octopus jokes, ink's in the air,
"Did you ask for a sketch? I'm beyond compare!"

Shells hide secrets, treasures of old,
A clam sings songs, if you dare be bold.
Just don't ask it to sing loud and clear,
It's more of a croak, with a hint of cheer!

Starfish applaud with their arms all wide,
Join the party, get swept in the tide.
In this realm of giggles, glimmers and schemes,
Laughter bubbles up, it's better than dreams!

## Glowing Trails of the Deep

Down below, where the colors burst,
Fish wear tuxedos, they're fancy first.
Anemones tickle with neon flair,
Who knew deep sea had its own millionaire?

Crabs throw confetti while they dance,
With every pinch, they take a chance.
A treasure chest filled with candy treats,
"Welcome aboard, it's your sugary feast!"

Glow-worms giggle in their bright parade,
Lighting up shadows, a prank they've made.
What's that in the current? Oh, just a boot,
Worn by a fish with a fancy flute!

Snails pull stunts, acrobatic delight,
Spinning around, they glimmer in flight.
Come join this circus, at the ocean's lap,
Where the antics are wild, and there's never a trap!

## Mystical Rays in the Marine Dark

Coral castles with windows aglow,
Mermaids gossip in currents below.
"Did you hear that?" a crab loves to tease,
Water tickles and bends like a breeze.

Anglerfish wink, with their lure so bright,
"Come a little closer, let's have a fright!"
But all they offer is laughter and cheer,
Their jokes are better, even under the pier!

Dolphins squeak in a dimly-lit race,
With a splashy smile, they're full of grace.
"Let's play peek-a-boo, don't swim away!"
In this hidden world, we frolic and play.

Stars twinkle from their watery throne,
As laughs echo through this place unknown.
Beneath the waves, the jokes never cease,
In the realm of giggles, we find our peace!

## Submerged Radiance

In the depths where the bright fishes gloat,
A lobster sings in a high-pitched note.
"Come swim with me, it's a wild jamboree!"
With a sparkle and twirl, it's a sight to see.

Lanterns float like dreams in the swell,
A fish floats by, with a wish to tell.
"Have you seen my socks? I lost them today,"
Underwater fashion, it's safe to say!

Bubble blasters shoot up in delight,
A parade of sea creatures, a funny sight.
Squids wear hats, clams sport bow ties,
Even the sharks can't help but rise!

So if you're down where the laughter's free,
Join the fish party, come swim with me.
In the glow of the ocean, fun lights the way,
Underwater antics are here to stay!

## Beneath the Silver Crest

Fish wear glasses to see what's near,
They giggle and whisper without any fear.
A crab does the cha-cha, all in a row,
While eels tell the jokes, stealing the show.

Shells bounce on bubbles, a rhythmic parade,
Sea horses jump in, their best moves displayed.
An octopus winks, with tentacles spinning,
In this underwater realm, everyone's winning!

A clownfish in stripes takes the stage with flair,
His friends laugh and cheer, but oh, what a scare!
A balloon floats by, drifting down from above,
They all chase it down, like a slippery love.

With fins all a-flutter, they dance and they sway,
Each creature a star in this watery play.
As bubbles burst laughter, their joy set alight,
In this realm of delight, what a glorious sight!

## **Chasing Glimmers in Silent Depths**

Bubbles pop loudly, sparking the thrill,
A turtle takes off, with extreme speed and skill.
A party of plankton starts doing a jig,
While a lonely old lobster grows tired of the dig.

Disco balls drift from the ships far above,
Tiny fish twirl, seeking fun that they love.
A stingray glides through, sporting shades with pride,
While a school swims by, all in perfect glide.

They spin 'round like tops, making waves with a splash,
Chasing the shimmer, they all make a dash.
A dolphin sings out, a melody bright,
As they flip and they flail in the warm, dusky night.

Amidst all the giggles and shimmering glee,
A seahorse yells out, "Come dance here with me!"
Together they laugh in this jovial show,
In the depths of the ocean, where happiness flows!

## The Deep's Secret Glow

Crabs wear party hats, feeling all grand,
As seabeans serve snacks from a velvety hand.
Turtles are jesters, flipping their tails,
While fish bop around with outrageous tales.

The seaweed sways like a goofy old friend,
Who tells all the jokes that just never end.
A dolphin's in charge of the music and beats,
As jellyfish groove on their gelatinous feats.

Starfish clap hands, although they have few,
They make quite the racket with what they can do.
A far-off squid zooms, wearing neon bright shoes,
While everyone laughs at the slip and the blues.

In this ocean of giggles, no sadness can dwell,
As laughter erupts like a wondrous spell.
The deep's secret glow shines with joy and grace,
In this wacky, wild, aquatic embrace!

## **Luminous Threads of Beneath**

A fish with a comb takes care of its scales,
While others gossip about their daily tales.
Squid in a tux, looking sharp as a whip,
Mimics the crab with a stutter and slip.

A chorus of shrimp serenades the night,
Creating a ruckus, what a glorious sight!
Anemones sway to the rhythm of fun,
As mermaids toss glitter, giggling and spun.

Dancing in circles, the starfish declare,
"Who needs the surface? We've got flair to spare!"
With bubbles for beats, they all shimmy and sway,
Making memories bright in their own underwater ballet.

Oh, what a party beneath the blue sea,
With laughter and joy, it's the place to be!
The glow of their giggles runs deep as the tide,
In this realm of delight, where all joy can abide!

**Neon Dreams of the Ocean Floor**

Deep below where fish do roam,
A disco ball made of foam.
Jellybeans swim and dance about,
While seaweed waves with a hearty shout.

Crabs wear shades and strut with flair,
Clams sing tunes in electric air.
Starfish wiggle, all decked in gold,
Grooving tales of legends told.

Turtles twist like they're in a race,
Lobsters spin in a silly chase.
Bubble-blowers make a scene,
As sea cucumbers bust a gleam.

In this realm, all jesters play,
With every flip, they steal the sway.
So dive right in, don't be too shy,
In neon dreams, the fish all fly.

## **Bioluminescent Serenade**

Oh, the bubbles, how they pop,
A glowing concert, never stop!
Pufferfish create a symphony,
While plankton join in harmony.

Sardines shimmer in a line,
Like a twinkling, sparkling vine.
The octopus, in glittered mood,
Jives with seaweed, quite the food!

Anemones sway, wearing crowns,
In ocean gowns of silken towns.
Each flicker winks and opens wide,
In this merry, aquatic slide.

So let us cheer, loud and clear,
For every glow, we hold so dear.
With laughter, glee, we serenade,
In the depths where dreams are played.

## Nymphs of the Liquid Light

Nymphs frolic in a twisty whirl,
With glittering tails that nicely twirl.
They toss and tumble, giggle and spin.
With laughter echoing deep within.

Their hair flows like strands of fine seaweed,
Each nymph a sparkle, a giggling bead.
Dancing with bubbles, they glide and sway,
Making fish grin in a crustacean ballet.

A dolphin joins, wears a toupee,
As nymphs declare it's a crazy day.
Seahorses laugh, add a little cheer,
While rays of sun adorn them near.

Oh, to be part of this swirling spree,
Where water's laughter sets your heart free.
So swim along, don't be apathetic,
Join the nymphs, jesters of the eclectic!

## **Beneath the Moonlit Tide**

Beneath the waves, where shadows play,
Octopuses dance in a merry ballet.
The moon hangs low, a giant cheese,
While fish munch on it, if you please.

Eels make faces, the joker type,
And clownfish style makes quite the hype.
A shark in shades, oh what a sight,
Zipping past with gleeful might.

Dancing kelp sways to the beat,
While sea turtles rock on their feet.
Giant squids throw confetti around,
In this underwater glow, laughter's found.

So heed the call, come join the crowd,
For fun and giggles, shout out loud!
In the depths where crabs have glee,
Life's a riot, just you and me.

## Chasing the Sea's Secret Illumination

Down below where bubbles bounce,
Fish wear hats that make us pounce.
Crabs are dancing, oh so spry,
While seaweed waves and jokes pass by.

A jellyfish in a tutu sways,
It twirls and spins in silly ways.
Octopus plays the accordion,
With every note, a new pun's born!

In coral castles, laughter flows,
A dolphin's joke? Nobody knows!
With every giggle, clams turn red,
As laughter echoes in their head.

So dive down deep, lose all your cares,
Join in the fun, there's joy everywhere!
Submarine's got the best of vibes,
A lantern fish steals laughs like tribes.

## Twilight's Embrace under Water

In twilight's glow, a fish takes flight,
It flashes scales, a silly sight.
With every swish, it tells a tale,
Of sea snails stealing each other's mail.

Starfish wear sunglasses, looking cool,
While turtles play at a swimming pool.
A seahorse prances, quite the tease,
Singing to shells with utmost ease.

The winky whale is quite the prank,
It hides behind reefs, a funny flank.
Bubbles rise with every joke,
While squids crack up and start to poke.

So dip your toes in waves of glee,
The ocean's stage is wild and free.
With every ripple, laughter rings,
As twilight wraps us in silly flings.

## Sirens of the Gleaming Abyss

In the depths of secrets, sirens sing,
With voices that make the sea creatures cling.
Mermaids giggle at a clumsy shark,
Who trips on coral like it's a lark.

Their hair made of kelp, they dance and twirl,
Spinning around like a whirlpool swirl.
"Catch me if you can!" they tease and glide,
While a crab tries to join in with pride.

Anemones tickle with soft, slippery quips,
As dolphins dive for joyous flips.
A treasure chest bursts at the seams,
Revealing gold doubloons and silly dreams.

So heed the call of these sparkling dames,
With jokes and riddles, they play their games.
In the gleaming abyss where fun begins,
The laughter of mermaids their sweet melody spins.

**Aquatic Twilight and Starry Breaches**

In twilight waters, stars collide,
With fish that wish they could take a ride.
A flounder rides a shooting star,
With giggles echoing near and far.

A crab with a bowtie thinks he's grand,
While sea otters hold a make-believe band.
The slugs on stage, they play their parts,
With melodies that tickle our hearts.

Lobsters whisper in a secret code,
Trading jokes on their clam shell road.
Each gurgle's a punchline, bubbling clear,
While every splash brings nothing but cheer.

So wade through waves where the laughter flows,
In twilight's arms, see how joy grows.
Where stars break through the watery dome,
Under the sea, we've found our home!

## Starry Breaches

The night sky winks as fish do prance,
With tiny stars that swim and dance.
An anglerfish starts the nightly show,
With puns and gags, he's the star we know.

A group of squids compose a tune,
While crabs chase shadows, beneath the moon.
They juggle shells with great finesse,
Creating laughs in a funny mess.

A whale's got jokes, but don't ask for one,
Because his punchlines take too long to run!
In waves of fun, we'll all take part,
As the sea holds secrets of laughter's art.

So dive down deep, in this watery realm,
Where friends and giggles take the helm.
Beneath the stars, what joy we find,
With silly fish and whimsical minds.

www.ingramcontent.com/pod-product-compliance
Lightning Source LLC
Chambersburg PA
CBHW060142230426
43661CB00003B/538